The Fellowship of the Rain

Poems by
Amarylis Douglas

BLUE LIGHT PRESS ◆ 1ST WORLD PUBLISHING

1ST WORLD
PUBLISHING

SAN FRANCISCO ◆ FAIRFIELD ◆ DELHI

Winner of the 2020 Blue Light Poetry Prize

The Fellowship of the Rain

Copyright ©2020 **Amarylis Douglas**

BLUE LIGHT PRESS
www.bluelightpress.com
bluelightpress@aol.com

1ST WORLD PUBLISHING
PO Box 2211
Fairfield, IA 52556
www.1stworldpublishing.com

BOOK & COVER PHOTO & DESIGN
Melanie Gendron
melaniegendron999@gmail.com

AUTHOR PHOTO
Ilmarinen Vogel

FIRST EDITION

ISBN: 978-1-4218-3661-4

The rain in Portland, Oregon is not just a weather condition, or an annoyance, or something from which to grow weary. To some, it may be any of those. But after living in the city for a while, one comes to realize that the rainy weather is slowly weaving itself into an all-encompassing fabric that unites you with different people in a common humanity. Children out at a rainy recess, wet soccer teams at practice, two young girls, heads together, chatting, under a big, black umbrella, a man, sitting in a window, playing his mandolin, sharing his music with all the people walking by down below: These are all members of the fellowship of the rain.

And especially, those, who know the rain most intimately: the men, women, children and animals who live on the streets, the homeless of the city. Each one is a poem.

"Sometimes the rain was beautiful. The lavender and silver streaks, gleaming in the mud, seek to be honored, to receive some words of gratitude."

Elizabeth Hardwick
From *Sleepless Nights*

Table of Contents

The Fellowship of the Rain

Here in the city, under the prayer of a streetlight,
the rain is your company, most of the night a soft chanting
on wet shoulders, cold hands, a pulled down knit cap.
You are grateful for the thankfully short conversation,
the burn of whiskey in your throat,
the momentary hallucination in the stretch of headlights
and for your home made of a sleeping bag and shopping cart.
Once there was a long table, three kinds of pie,
plenty of family to go around, to hold you in, tie you down.
All you had to do was to listen.
Here in the city, under the halo of a streetlight
you know what a Thanksgiving night smells like.
Although you will sleep alone tonight,
you now belong to the fellowship of the rain.

Castles in the Air

Three young men, twenties, thirties, standing around
in tee shirts, next to a line of blue tarp houses,
kicking some leaves around, kicking some schemes around,
up, into the damp December air under the Hawthorne bridge.
Round blue homes, built on cold cement,
tucked in tight at the corners at night.
The village stretches three blocks.
(One green fir branch stuck in a post. A thin red ribbon,
celebrating Christmas, unraveling in the wind.)
One night a single tarp was turned into a house.
Later, it became a line of good ideas,
then this village under the Hawthorne bridge,
just up river from the latest gentrification.
Grace is nearby, just out of reach. Grace is reclaimed
on these wet city streets every morning,
lost again to the needs of the night.
There is a kind mist out this winter. The smell of a rainforest
permeates this blue tarp village, built in a rain forest,
built in a city, a city that keeps breathing warm promises
into these castles in the air.

Waiting for his Dad

He was an island kid,
went to birthday parties, swung on tire swings,
ran around barefoot, grew up in the breeze of the ocean,
swam in the salt of the sea, became a most beautiful boy,
auburn-haired, easy going.
He cried alone in the afternoons, as the light
slanted through his bedroom window.
He waited for his dad.
At fifteen, he ran away to the city,
found some friends on a corner, joined a familiar conversation.
In the afternoons, in the slant of the light, it was an easy
slip into oblivion. He sold or gave away everything but his backpack,
two books, a change of clothes, a picture of his dad.
He became a handsome member of the fellowship of the rain.
It all seemed easier on the street. Every afternoon
until it wasn't easy any more.
The change of clothes was gone, his two books,
only the picture in his pocket when they found him
curled up on the wet brown bench, waiting for his dad.

Bundles and Bags

a guy who loves dancing

You wear high-water, skinny black pants, white socks,
push your shopping cart, bundles and bags.
You slide
onto center stage, under the misty street light.
The Saturday night scene has just ended.
Your slim shadow glides across city cement.
Jazz melodies hum in your ears, reminders of before.
Over to the trash can, you pick through for
thrown out food, or discarded inspiration.
Too young to be on the street, too sensitive to not.
You speak intimately to a closed-store, window mannequin,
sidle up to the ATM, the brief distraction of money,
return to the music
your legs, your shoulders, your feet.

You can take away the writer's pen
but you cannot stop the words pushing in his throat.

You are rising to your crescendo,
long legs of Fred Astaire, just, almost, out of control
familiar rhythms worn into your soul,
set free again, you are back,
red satin shirt, shiny black jacket
on stage, under the lights, inside the music.
You are the music,
dancing your shopping cart on up the street.

Sweet Girl

Sweet girl in a long brown corduroy skirt
wide eyes, brown bangs.
You remind me of my daughter.
I want to hug you, bring you home,
offer you dinner, a bedroom, a choice...
a reason
not to sleep out on the street
in the rain.
I try to talk to you like a mother.
All you will accept is my five-dollar bill.

Your Brother

Last night you made up your bed under a beveled glass window.
The door to the church was locked.
You laid down your cardboard, your memory-foam,
climbed in under that blue plaid blanket.
For a while you just lay there, watched the stars
listened to them hum, out into the black October sky.
You wondered about heaven.

You dreamed of you and your little brother.
You two were sitting on the kitchen stoop
counting the stars,
counting out smooth brown chestnuts into a grocery bag
chill coming into your noses, dinner bubbling inside.
Two young brothers with matching crewcuts
under that yellow back porch light.

A Pink Blanket

He hugged you, brought you home.
Together you made big plans.
You dreamed of a family. He wanted to be
a family-man, a man. You fell in love.
even when he cursed you, struck you down.
His fists, hard against your little face.
His words, deafening in your frightened ears.
Again, again, sometimes for no reason, until
you thought, he was probably right.
You were not worth anything, a poor excuse.
Then you saw that pink blanket. You remembered
you were once a perfect, a loveable child.
You grabbed that blanket and ran. You ran
out into the night. You ran.
You grabbed that blanket and ran.
Your breath caught in your throat. You ran
with little baby bits of some kind of courage.
You left behind everything you had lost.
In the morning, in the rain, a pink blanket
dropped by the curb.

Handsome

Black wool topcoat, black knit cap
thick silver curls cut crisp, stylish, handsome,
spilling words in spasms, to everyone, anyone, no one,
tidy, red backpack, cashmere scarf,
talking to yourself, answering, jitters,
talking to your past,
working it out, walking it out,
sometimes just shaking, short bursts of shaking.
You tilt your head like a bird listening for a worm.
You look up, head into Safeway,
come back out with two cups of coffee,
one for you, one for a friend.

The Split Rail Fence

On a city street in Portland, Oregon
a long line of bent shadows wait for a space for the night.
On the corner, a fire in a trash can shoots sparks into the sky.
Across the street, a solitary young fellow sets up in a doorway.
He tries to fall asleep with his eyes open.

Back in Madison, Wisconsin
she carries his picture in her brown leather wallet.
He was ten, good looking already,
bashful brown eyes from under an oversized white cowboy hat
fringed vest, pearl-button shirt, leaning against the split rail fence.
She had given him and his sister more love by herself
than two parents could together.
She doesn't try to call anymore, doesn't say his name
to her new husband. They have a good life,
tailgate parties up at Green Bay in the fall,
sitting out on the porch on summer nights,
like tonight. Moonlight makes shadows in the front yard
lays open the heart of the night.
She looks out to the split rail fence.

The Conductor

As I drove by the park today, I saw a man in a tall black hat,
tails, flapping lapels, red ascot at his neck,
red cummerbund around his belly, a proud bird.
He directed an invisible orchestra, a symphony of pleasure.
He hit sweet pianissimos, built to bold crescendos.
I watched his glory, his pride, his moment of splendor,
this man of passion.
The crowd across the street, waiting for the bus
did not look over.

There are so many men of passion
who walk around the city.

The light changed. I drove on, but came back later for more.
The crowd across the street had gone. I recognized the Conductor,
now bent over, bundled up in a sparrow brown sweater,
weaving his way up the sidewalk.
On the grass, under a tree, his plumage was left in a pile.

Coyote Eyes

Dark mud leaves stuck thick to this November street.
Shivering damp stray, rocking on his haunches. Wary, wiry
crouched inside his dripping doorway lair.
Wild brown hair, tied still in the wind. Coyote eyes
lost on a city corner.
Now comes a long inhale — marijuana.
Breathing. Soon. Pale blue, the sky blows holes
in heavy gray nimbus.
Later, at sunset, light pink escaping around the edges.

Dreaming

In the cool of the city morning, before the burn of the day,
before the nighttime dreams become embers,
you are in a little park, on a quiet corner,
on a square patch of grass, near a gentle bubbling fountain,
stretched out, long and lean, young and unknowing,
new to the city, no sleeping bag, no tent,
not yet pushing a shopping cart,
Totally free,
your hands, a prayer pillow under your head, your socks,
tucked in tidy,
each into its own clean, white, high-top sneaker.

Justice (Just Is)

Just another home built in a doorway,
made of a shopping cart, a tarp,
and all the damp possessions you can carry.

Just another kid in between his drug dreams,
"Will you tell them I'm OK?"
then notices we had given him a twenty.

Just two young sisters on the road, snuggling
together in that dirty, flowered comforter,
dreaming of the springtime, before the beatings.

Just another hungry guy, trying to squeeze his fingers
into a parking meter, for some forgotten change,
then into the trash can for some dinner, a partly-smoked cigarette.

Just another mother sitting on a blanket,
holding her Baby Jesus on her lap.
A few dollars in her paper bag.

Just another Thursday evening in December.
Just another city, just another town.
Justice
(Just is.)
Some get left behind.

Her Silhouette

In the middle of the rain, in the middle of the street
in the middle of Saturday afternoon,
face to face. I smile. You throw your words at me
like dirt, words about a mother. They sting.
I run so fast. I try to not look back, in case,
I must. You are gone. I am gone.
You do not remember me or that today
Is Saturday.
You were
a little boy, snuggled up beneath
your mother's silhouette. She held you in her lap.
You smelled her heart.
Then she was gone. Near, then gone, then gone.
You cried until your tears turned to rage. Your words
filled with fire, a fire beneath your heart.

This afternoon I came too close. To you, I had no eyes.

Pretty

I noticed your umbrella first, full open circle of color,
a twirl of pastels, a pretty rooftop over your yellow comforter.
The rain began to fall again.
There is so much more trash this winter,
Left-behind shirts, muddied socks, a sneaker,
How does someone forget a sneaker?
left under bar-lit overhangs, late night hangouts.
You had remembered everything. Your housekeeping, tidy.
Your home for the night, in the same doorway as last night,
I saw you last night
right down the street from the Mani/Pedi shop,
the happy hour bar, the moody, red-draped fondue restaurant.
In a city full of umbrellas, yours is the prettiest.
You never looked up, never spoke or nodded.
Your clothes were folded in a pile, neatly. Your shoes,
set beside them, neatly.
Your clothes were clean, your hair, brushed.
In this dirty doorway of this vacant store,
you were smiling, setting up house for the night.
In the morning, you were gone.

Down Burnside*

Morning drive down Burnside, toward the river,
the bridge, there you were, a young fellow,
just climbed out of your sleeping bag,
from under a rain wet tarp,
in the doorway of an empty store.
I was stopped at the red light, so I watched.
Handsome boy, late teens, early twenties,
just crawled out of his home to sit inside a doorway,
rain coming straight down.
You sit and eat some crackers, breakfast.
A son, my son, your son,
new to the streets, maybe his first night,
brand new sleeping bag, could have been a Christmas present.
You crawled out from under a tarp
into the fellowship of the rain.

---

*Burnside is a street that runs through the heart
of Portland, Oregon. It divides north and south.

16

Barefoot Priest

Satisfied
with your reflection in the wet, streetcar window,
dark, clean, handsome. You step off
to your usual corner by the Safeway entrance,
mumbling prayers to yourself,
to any of your gods or visions.
Huge, heavy, blue wool blanket, wrapped
around your shoulder, hangs down,
almost to the street.
Hunchback Buddha, barefoot priest
standing in the city snow.

I fumble in my bag for some coins,
dare a look into the mystery
of those holy hazel eyes.
But you are not asking for money.
"Happy Christmas," you offer,
then put your hands together in a blessing.

Under a Halo

Violet light slips down from heaven onto the Rose City*.
The last sunlight of the day reflects off the side of Big Pink**.
It forces your tired eyes into a squint, your mouth into a smile.
A day well done, a course well played, choices well made,
You must be proud.

Proud, you left your spot clean this morning,
as the sun first spread like warm taffy,
under the Hawthorne bridge***.
You took your time, rolled up your sleeping bag, picked up
the left-over dinner wrappers. No circle of trash left behind
to give the homeless a bad name.

Proud, how you balanced those overstuffed black bags,
full of cans, on your bicycle handlebars,
rode to the Quality market, traded them in for a slip of paper
that bought you a bag of chips, turkey roll-up and a Coke.

Proud, when you relaxed your tightening fists,
refused to listen, when an argument heated up
between the street families,
down at the river. You kept you head down, just kept walking.
No one even knew you were there.

Proud, you took only one hit
from the girl leaning against the Walgreens
with the peace sign on her backpack, dreadlocks on her shoulders,
when she invited you over with her slow brown eyes.

Proud, as you sit here now, on this curb,
in the last warmth of the day.
Light vanishes. The violet turns dark. You find yourself again
under the halo of a streetlight,
on a corner, of the city you love, in the beginning mist of the night.

---

*Rose City: a name for Portland, Oregon
**Big Pink: A tall pink building in Portland
***Hawthorne bridge: One of the bridges that cross the Willamette
river in Portland

Street Pirate

Skinny, disheveled,
black bandana fallen down
over one eye, toothless grin,
your backpack slung, cavalier,
over your shoulder.
You walk by the café window. Shoot
a fast side glance in at my lunch.

Hungry, diminished,
but with a step still full of pride
and purpose.

You Wait

The apple trees are dropping white sachets into left-over puddles.
The crowd is lined up, outside, down the street.
Spring ritual, ice cream after dinner.
You stand taller than the crowd.
Gray eyes, you look past this deciduous crowd
out to the west hills.
You, the silent pitch pine, hold your sign,
"Homeless. Anything helps."
The crowd is anxious.
You are perfect, street worn, lissome,
your long brown beard, tangled.
Perfect in your humble patience,
your polite hunger, your brief request.
No one looks longer than a glance.
You look out, over the crowd, this April street this city,
to the sweet pine forest. You smell the apple sachet.
You wait.

Bumps

The city has grown bumps.
They have popped up in the park,
along the river, in the middle of the sidewalk,
in a vacant doorway, under the damp dripping roofs.
Gray, brown, blue, camouflage, single round mounds
or multi-shaped, family bumps,
pieces of insulation,
humiliation, sticking out the side,
a metal shopping cart nearby, sometimes
a neighboring bump, or two,
homes for the night, the new American landscape.

Blue Eyes Looking West

You are here, leaning against the side of the Walgreens
most afternoons around three,
dry, under the dripping overhang.
Your blue eyes looking west, over the Steele bridge, out
across sunset highway to the coast.
Sometimes you laugh with friends. Sometimes you sleep.
You dream back East to the baseball field, behind the fire station,
The lineup on the bench,

ten boys, summer crewcuts, sunburned necks
you, the chosen one, the favorite.
your coach, your mentor, your predator, your user
your abuser.
his cigarette ash about to fall.
You bite your lip so hard it bleeds.
You want to run   *far*
west,
past the sun that heats that ball field,
past the shame, the smell of grassy innocence.

Forty years later, in the West, you are here, in this new lineup.
The sidewalk fills with beer cans and hamburger wrappers.
The clouds block out the sun. Rain drips down the overhang.
You have come. You have found a place
in the cool comfort of the fellowship of the rain.

"Every little bit helps. God bless you."

You sit on the sidewalk behind a thin blue blanket
in front of the coffee shop, at all the coffee drinkers' feet.
Your water color paintings for sale, the memories of a veteran,
explosions of lights, blasts that burn long after
in your ears, leave a permanent dryness in your mouth,
soft portraits of your friends who put their lives
on the line for you and you, for them,
their squinting blue eyes, empty brown stares,
mid-western accents, southern drawls,
sweaty mud skin, ashen fright,
their pictures of their girlfriends, their little brothers,
their parents' worry, their parents' pride.
Stolen right in front of you.
You sit behind a thin blue cloth on a white paint bucket,
memories for sale. A sign propped up. "Have a nice day."
You are homeless. You are a vet.

This Morning

In honor of Mt Hood, the great snowy peak,
that watches over the city of Portland, Oregon

I saw an old man stash his shopping cart
behind the bus stop at SE 39th and Powell.
He hoped no one would steal his bundle of clothes,
while he searched out just one more fix.
He looked up to the great father mountain
that keeps watch over his city.

I saw a skinny man ride his bicycle, balance
his black trash bags, already filling with empty cans.
He smelled that April morning
cooling in the bakery window. Then he rode on
under the watch of the great father mountain
that keeps watch over his city.

I dreamed of a pretty, blue-eyed girl,
who woke early this morning, just before her baby.
She looked out through the dust
on the women's shelter window, out, to a different life
she saw for her baby. She prayed to the great father mountain
that keeps watch over his city.

Jazz

Inside the dark lounge, a few couples oscillate
around the dim-lit floor. Brass jazz men melodize.
Across from a small round table,
red velvet drapes frame the stars.
Outside, at the corner, November soul man
pours his heart into his old sax
with so much tenderness, the busy city people stop,
drop a five into his case.
White moonlight shines its spell down onto the cold city street.
The stars begin to sway.

Somehow

Somehow you are headed back into the train station
just before the rains begin again.
If you can just make it through those florescent lights,
then down, into the deep comfort, that familiar dark hallway,
slumped mounds of clothing, untied shoes, backpacks, dropped.
You slide your back down against the cool wall.
Your back is aching. Your eyes, already heavy.
Your captor whispers love songs into your ears.
You lean back. You lean back, relieved, against the cool
cement wall, the words still dripping into your ears.
Slower motion, your head nods, you fall onto a pillow,
Colorless, effortless, barefoot, dewy grass.
Celestial dust settles around you.
You don't hear the whistle alert,
the engine's moan, deep in its belly,
as it pushes out into the rain, through
the streets, the city, up into the hills,
back into your old neighborhood.
You stay behind.

This Night

Another car tonight, another wake-up rap on the window
to startle you out of your dream.
It's a cold, damp night out there,
no one left to catch you up, to warm you with compassion,
to notice that you finally "hit your bottom," tonight
on this city street. At last it's your turn
to receive the "gift of grace," to taste the brief
sweetness of humility, to understand that the cold clink of coins
dropped in your hand, or even a few extra bills
can buy dog food for your pit bull, your buddy,
your scrawny protector from the "families" of the street,
families of children, washed
in the same gray-green city mud that you know the smell of,
children camped on the corners of the day, thieving
violators of the night, children who don't bother anymore
to stand in endless lines of "not enough,"
for the chance at a handout or a night's sleep on a dirty,
wooden floor. You had a family once,
you loved them with all your heart, when
you could find your way to the belief in love,
the belief in being worthy.

Now you have come down to "no way out."
You have found there is a peace there in the knowing
that they, your family, with wet eyes and aching hearts,
have tried to move on with their lives. No one is here to notice
tonight, as you "Please exit the vehicle Sir."
but instead of picking through your backpack of hard-luck stories
and excuses,
instead, you look up
beyond the heavy clouds of blame and regret,

out into the forgiving black sky,
and to the stars, to a once familiar belief in these stars,
that silently witness this night,
and welcome you into the fellowship of the rain.

Christmas Eve

Born of the spirit of Lewis and Clark,
fueled by a thousand artists. Scientists came over the hills
to this Willamette valley, watched over by the great white-haired
Godfather, kindly grandmother, who reaches up
to poke a hole into heaven.
Here, where houses full of glass hang off the sides of mossy cliffs,
where some people live in luxury, among
the ancient stories of the whispering firs,
where too many others, down below,
push cold metal shopping carts, filled with their own stories,
mental illness, addiction, abuse,
poverty, loneliness, "down on your luck"
into the eventual evening to sleep like bums, like bumps
under wet covers, in the middle of the rain,
in the middle of the street, in the middle of Christmas eve,
in the middle of this epidemic,
in the middle of all the passers-by.

Under the Light

The rain has been falling all afternoon.
As night begins, the moon is just now slipping out
from behind the afternoon clouds.
A short man with a long, dark pony tail,
beat up sneakers, wet grey sweat shirt
pushes his cart in front of me, up to the street corner.
He stops for the light, hikes up his rope-belted pants.
I rush up behind him, avoiding puddles, to not be late
to meet friends for dinner and a movie we have been wanting to see.
But today I stop. I watch this little man. Then, for some reason
I look up, maybe to try again to find that man who lives in the moon.
I can't find him. But he shines his light down onto the wet streets
of this city,
into the puddles, in through the restaurant windows.
His shines down a holy light, onto this man waiting at the corner.
It glorifies him. It glorifies each of his shadows that walk around
down here below.

Hope

You are alone tonight, just you and your dog and your backpack,
sitting under this city bridge, trucks and cars rumbling over.
The rain is falling straight down, just beyond your sneakers.
You spent the afternoon right outside Trader Joe's, holding
your cardboard sign that ended with "Thank You. Have a nice day"
and began with "Homeless. Please help."
So many shoppers hurried faster into the store when they saw you.
They stared uncomfortably straight ahead
or suddenly needed to check their phones.
One looked briefly into your face, rushed inside
then turned around, came back out
to drop some change into your wet hands,
hands still soft with naivete, eyes still wide with fear,
memories still nightmares, a heart still open to some kind of hope.
Maybe there are friends set up under this same bridge. Maybe
they would welcome you to sleep beside their fire.
Maybe they would listen, if you could start
to tell them.

Epilogue

On this night

On this night the wind swept the city clean.
The streetlights trembled at the horrible-grand
job of replacing the stars. The rains came,
again and again, down
onto the row of tarp houses,
onto the backs, bent over a fire in a trash can,
into the dreams of the children, snuggled
into their parents' sins and heartache.

As the rains began to lessen, the cool, steady
drip of absolution fell down onto all
the members of the fellowship of the rain.

About the Author

Amarylis Douglas is originally from the Berkshires, in western Massachusetts. She has lived for forty years on the island of Martha's Vineyard, where she brought up her three children and taught in the island schools. She also lived in Portland, Oregon for ten years, where she worked in the Title One program for Portland Public Schools. She has been in many writing groups in all three areas, most recently The Martha's Vineyard Poets' Collective. Now back, based on the island, she returns often to spend time in Portland. Her poetry was first published in *Our Place, A Selection of New England Poets*, and also in "The Vineyard Gazette" and "The Martha's Vineyard Times."

CPSIA information can be obtained
at www.ICGtesting.com
Printed in the USA
LVHW091043280820
664155LV00006B/992